Will It Be Okay?

by Crescent Dragonwagon

Pictures by Ben Shecter

Harper & Row, Publishers

New York, Hagerstown, San Francisco, London

This story was written during the Intensive Journal Workshop led by Dr. Ira Progoff, held at the Vallombrosa Center in Menlo Park, California, in August 1976. The author would like to express her gratitude to all who were present, for each in some way made possible this story.

WILL IT BE OKAY?
Text copyright © 1977 by Crescent Dragonwagon
Illustrations copyright © 1977 by Ben Shecter
For information address Harper & Row, Publishers, Inc., 10 East 53rd Street, New York, N.Y. 10022. Published simultaneously in Canada by Fitzhenry & Whiteside Limited, Toronto.

Library of Congress Cataloging in Publication Data
Dragonwagon, Crescent.

    Will it be okay?
    SUMMARY: A mother comforts a child about her special fears concerning dogs, thunder, snakes, and other things.
    [1. Fear—Fiction]   I. Shecter, Ben.
II. Title.
PZ7.D7824Whm   [E]   76-48859
ISBN 0-06-021737-5
ISBN 0-06-021738-3 lib. bdg.

To the One who's always with us,
whispering "It's okay!"
this book is humbly and lovingly offered.

"Will it be okay?"

"Yes, it will."

"But what if a big dog comes?"
"You will know whether it is friendly or not.
If it is friendly,
you run your fingers
through its thick brown-and-white fur.

If it is not friendly,
you stand perfectly still and unafraid,
and it stops barking, and comes to you,
and sits quietly beside you."

"But what if there is thunder and lightning?"
"You sit at your window
and watch the rain beating down
over the houses and fields
in the dark night.
You see how special it is,
because the lightning
shows the rainy sky and countryside and all the city.
You pay attention
because the loud thunder is calling you,
saying:
   Look, look!
   The world is receiving a deep long drink!"

"But what if there is snow, lots and lots of snow?"
"You put on your red leggings and your brown boots,
and your pink coat, and your plaid scarf,
and your yellow hat, and your green earmuffs,
and two pairs of striped mittens,
one on top of the other."

"But what if snakes come in the night?"
"You keep a flute by your bed and play a song,
and the snakes hear,
and are quiet, and happy, and love you."

"But what if the cabbages don't come up?"
"We drive to the nursery,
and we buy seven tomato plants, just in case.
When we come home, we dig seven holes in the garden,
and put a tomato plant in each one.
We pat the earth back around each tomato plant,
and pour a bucket of water around each one.
Then we go inside to read a book.

When we come out again,
there is a tiny row of cabbage seedlings."

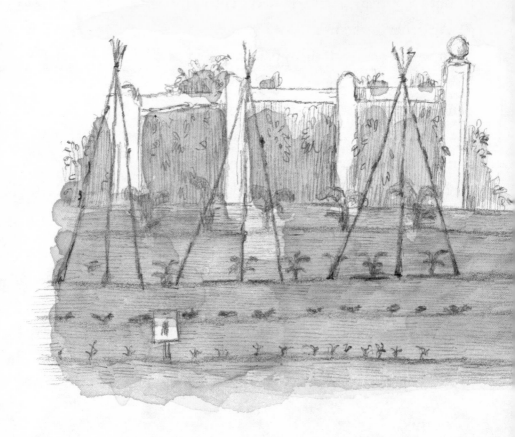

"But what if I hate everyone?"
"You run away.
You pack raisins, walnuts, oranges, crackers,
and a flashlight in a red bandanna.
You knot its four corners together,
and tie it to a stick, and carry it over your shoulder.

You walk and walk till you come to the park.

You stay all afternoon,
sitting by yourself under a tree.

When you come home again, you don't hate everyone."

"But what if someone hates me?"

"You feel lonely and sad.

You walk and walk until you come to a small pond.

You kneel in the grass by the edge of this pond,

and you see something move.

You put out your hand, and a tiny frog,

no bigger than your thumbnail, hops into it.

Very carefully, you lift your hand up to your ear,

and the frog whispers:

Other people love you.

Maybe that person will love you again, maybe not.

In any case, it is all right.

Because a frog tells you this, you believe it."

"But what if I forget my lines in the Thanksgiving play?"
"You make up new ones then and there.
And later, everyone will say:

What a wise and sensible child!
She forgot her lines, so she made up new ones!"

"But what if nobody likes the way I dance?"
"You go dancing in the woods,
alone in the crackling leaves.
One day you meet someone else dancing in the woods.
You dance together.
You throw leaves on each other,
you lie down in the leaves.

Then you go home and draw pictures,
and drink cocoa with whipped cream."

"But what if a bee stings me?"
"You run to the kitchen
and I rub a piece of raw onion
back and forth on the sting.
You say:

A piece of onion? That is silly!

That won't work!
But it does."

"But what if you die?"

"My loving doesn't die.
It stays with you,
as warm as two pairs of mittens on top of each other.
When you remember you and me, you say:
    What can I do with so much love?
    I will have to give some away.

So you love thunder and lightning,
dogs, snakes, snow, and planting cabbages.
You dance with other people in the leaves,
and are in plays with them and run away with them.
You love them, and they love you,
and you eat raisins together."

"So it will be okay?"
"Yes, my love, it will."